CHILDREN'S LIT.

PRINGLE

Wolfman

DATE DUE			
MAY 17			
MAR 16		NOV 13 2009	
NOV 14			
MAY 1			
NOV 08			

QL
737
.C22
P957

Missouri Western State College Library
St. Joseph, Missouri

841060

Wolfman

WOLFMAN

Exploring the World of Wolves

LAURENCE PRINGLE

Charles Scribner's Sons NEW YORK

Illustration Credits:
Fred H. Harrington, 59; courtesy of L. David Mech, 7, 8, 16, 23, 25, 27, 33, 38, 54, 56, National Film Board of Canada, 3; Laurence Pringle, frontispiece, 11, 13, 17, 20, 30, 35, 40, 42, 44, 48, 52, 63, 65.

Maps by Jackie Aher

Copyright © 1983 Laurence Pringle

Library of Congress Cataloging in Publication Data
Pringle, Laurence P.
Wolfman / exploring the world of wolves.
Bibliography: p.
Includes index.
Summary: A career biography of the wildlife biologist who has spent twenty-five years studying the wolf.
1. Wolves—Juvenile literature. [1. Mech, L. David.
2. Biologists. 3. Wolves] I. Title.
QL737.C22P74   1983   599.74′442′0924 [B] [92]   82-19144
ISBN 0-684-17832-X

This book published simultaneously in the
United States of America and in Canada -
Copyright under the Berne Convention.
All rights reserved. No part of this book
may be reproduced in any form without the
permission of Charles Scribner's Sons.

1 3 5 7 9 11 13 15 17 19 Q/C 20 18 16 14 12 10 8 6 4 2

Printed in the United States of America

Contents

1. Of Wolves and Wolfmen   1
2. The Lure of Wildness   5
3. To See a Wolf   10
4. Further Adventures on Isle Royale   19
5. Thunder and Lightning   29
6. Radio Tracking and Wolf Number 2407   37
7. Exploring Wolf Territories   47
8. Keeping Watch   58

   Further Reading   66
   Index   69

1 Of Wolves and Wolfmen

Wolf. For many people this word means something to fear—a dangerous animal, savage, cruel, bloodthirsty. The Beast. These feelings were born long ago. They can be traced to Europe in the Middle Ages, a time of deep ignorance and superstition. It was a time to believe in all sorts of fanciful things—vampires, ghosts, and ferocious packs of wolves that chased people as they traveled by horse-drawn sleighs through the winter night. The wolf was feared as a creature of darkness and as a tool of the Devil by people who had no firsthand experience with the animal and wanted none, except to kill it.

European settlers brought these feelings about the wolf to North America. They and their descendants killed wolves by the thousands because, at times, it was necessary to protect livestock but also because it *felt* right to kill an animal they judged to be evil and worthless. Even today these feelings are stirred in some people when they hear the word *wolf.*

Wolf. For other people this word means something to admire—an animal that is the ancestor of our dogs and that has many qualities we appreciate in these pets and in ourselves. An animal that is cooperative, playful, intelligent, and fiercely loyal. Not The Beast but Brother Wolf.

Like feelings of fear and hate, this attitude about the wolf was born long ago. Indians and Eskimos who hunted had deep respect for other hunters—bears, eagles, wolves. And the wolf was a great hunter. To have the endurance and prowess of the wolf was an ideal that Eskimo and Indian hunters strived for but felt they could never achieve.

These feelings were based on firsthand knowledge, on observations of real wolves, not on fearful fantasies. Nevertheless, the feelings of Indians about the wolf, and about all of nature, were not respected by European settlers. The wisdom and values of native North Americans, like the "savages" themselves, were devalued and trampled on.

During most of the history of the United States, people killed wolves and felt self-righteous about it. By the early 1900s the wolf was gone from nearly all of its former range, which had extended from Mexico to the Arctic, and from the Northeast to the Pacific Northwest. Not until the early 1930s was the wolf given protection in some national parks. And then hunters claimed that wolves within the boundaries of Alaska's Mount McKinley National Park (now called Denali Park and Preserve) should be killed in order to protect caribou and other game animals.

So, in the spring of 1939, a biologist was assigned to study the wolves of Mount McKinley. Adolph Murie was the first scientist to undertake serious research on the wolf. He could truthfully write that "scarcely anything was known about the wolf's home life or his relationship to mountain sheep, caribou, moose, or other smaller species."

Adolph Murie spent parts of three years hiking and skiing in the vast national park. During six months of 1939 he walked more than 1,700 miles. He observed wolves whenever possible but learned about them in other ways, too. He collected and examined thousands of wolf droppings. These scats, as they are called, contained undigested hair and bits of bone, and revealed what the wolves ate. Adolph Murie also searched for the skulls of mountain sheep. He found more than eight hundred, and from the amount of tooth wear on their jawbones learned the age of the sheep. He found that mountain sheep in the prime of life seldom died. He concluded that mostly young, old, or diseased sheep had been killed by wolves.

Until Adolph Murie began the first serious study of the wolf, little was known about the relationships between wolves and such prey as these caribou.

Murie also searched for wolf dens. In mid-May 1940, after a fresh snowfall, he saw wolf prints near a cabin where he was staying. He followed the prints for about a mile to a bluff overlooking a river and discovered a den. The parent wolves ran off, but stayed near, barking and howling. Murie heard pups whimpering within the den. He feared that the parents would move the pups and that he would fail to find the new location. "I could not make matters much worse," Murie wrote, "so I wriggled into the burrow."

About twelve feet from the entrance he found a chamber where six pups squirmed. He brought three of them out of the burrow in order to examine them in the light. They appeared to be only about a week old; their eyes had not yet opened. Murie crawled into the den again and returned two of the pups. He took one pup home to raise and study, although he felt guilty about disturbing the wolf family.

To Murie's surprise and delight, the parent wolves did not move their remaining pups. He found a good observation point, and for nearly two months he watched the home life of an Alaskan wolf family.

Adolph Murie had supposed that the wolf family would be made up of the pups and their two parents. Instead, five adults cared for the pups. Food was brought to the mother and the pups by the other adult wolves. A female stayed with the pups during the few times the mother was away hunting.

Murie was struck by the sharing and cooperation among members of the wolf pack. "The strongest impression remaining with me after watching the wolves on numerous occasions was their friendliness," Murie wrote. "The adults were friendly toward each other and amiable toward the pups."

All too soon, in the summer of 1941, Murie's study ended. His written report, *The Wolves of Mount McKinley,* is still a classic of careful observation and skillful writing. It gave the world a far different view of the wolf than was held by most people.

Murie's pioneer work began to separate the real wolf from its folklore. He inspired others to learn more. Since the early 1940s several biologists have studied wolves in the wild—in Alaska, Canada, Michigan's Isle Royale, Minnesota, and, most recently, in Italy. Adolph Murie was the first of these wolfmen, as they are sometimes called. Other wolfmen have contributed to our growing understanding of the wolf. All of them would probably agree, however, that the efforts and accomplishments of one man stand out. Dave Mech, whose name rhymes with "each," has so far spent twenty-five years studying the wolf.

More than any other person, Dave Mech *is* wolfman. This book is about him.

2 The Lure of Wildness

On a June morning in 1958, Dave Mech found himself in the footsteps of Adolph Murie. He was not in Alaska but on an island—Isle Royale National Park, which lies in Lake Superior. Yet Dave Mech was beginning a study of wolves just as Murie had nineteen years earlier, hiking mile after mile in wolf country, collecting scats, seeking a rare glimpse of a wolf.

On that two-hundred-ten-square-mile island there were many miles to hike in solitude, and many hours to think. Mech thought about the wolf—still largely an animal of mystery—and about all of the questions he wanted to answer. At times on the trail he probably wondered, as people do in good or bad situations: How did I ever get *here?*

Part of the answer, he knew, lay back in Syracuse, New York, where he was born in 1937. Dave Mech's interest in the outdoors was certainly influenced by his father, who enjoyed fishing and who took the family camping. Both of his parents fostered in him a love for learning. About the time Adolph Murie was watching wolf pups in Alaska, five-year-old Dave Mech was given one of his first books, *American Wildlife*.

"I can still remember certain pictures in that book—the bison, the bald eagle. Later, in school, I read anything I could get my hands on about wilderness—*We Took to the Woods, Jeff White: Young Woods-*

man, books about outdoor survival. Northern wilderness fascinated me. I sought books about the far north, not about tropical jungles."

At the age of eleven, Dave Mech "exaggerated" his age in order to join the Boy Scouts and increase his opportunities for outdoor adventure. He and his friends found patches of wildness in the city of Syracuse. They caught snakes from fields and salamanders from ponds. And there was a great bare hill, surrounded by houses, that at times seemed like a wild mountain. "During a snowstorm I would trek around on Hunt's Hill. With a sky full of snow blotting out the city, I could imagine that I was exploring the Arctic tundra."

Yet, if you had asked young Dave Mech what he wanted to be, his answer would have been: astronomer. For several years he kept a notebook of astronomy observations and clippings. Looking back, Mech now realizes that he wanted to be a scientist, and the science of astronomy was the only one he knew about. He did not know that a person could be a biologist. That idea came to him at the age of fourteen, during a one-week camp session in 1950.

That summer, Dave Mech and several other members of his Boy Scout troop were chosen to attend a conservation education camp in the Catskill Mountains. The staff included a college student whose major at Cornell University was wildlife biology. It was a revelation to Dave Mech that a person could actually have such a career. He tucked his astronomy notebook away and vowed to attend Cornell to learn about wildlife.

Mech was also powerfully influenced at that camp by another experience, when professional trappers demonstrated ways of catching fur-bearing mammals. "Trapping was less controversial then than it is now," Mech says. "For me, then and now, the appeal of trapping has little or nothing to do with killing an animal."

Mech learned that he could probably catch furbearers within walking distance of his home. "It was a tremendous revelation to me, and right away I began reading magazines and books about trapping. In the autumn I bought some traps and began. My first catch was a gray fox.

While a teenager, Dave Mech (left) posed with a friend and a wild mink they had caught. His interest in carnivorous animals led Mech to study wildlife biology.

"At that time, trapping was what I wanted to do more than anything else. It was done outdoors in wild places. And in order to be successful I had to know a lot about the animals I was trying to catch. This is part of the mystique of trapping.

"In a sense I was already on my way to becoming a wildlife biologist—not just reading about animals but interpreting tracks and other signs, learning about their lives. And the trapping literature made it clear that carnivores were special. Anyone could catch muskrats, but mink, foxes, and other predators were wary and a real challenge to outwit. They were the 'intellectuals' of the furbearers. They fascinated me, and I suppose those early trapping experiences clinched the matter—that someday I would study carnivores."

In 1954, accepted as a student at Cornell University, Mech began studying zoology, ornithology, mammalogy, and all of the other "ologies" that lead to a degree in wildlife biology. He supported himself by working thirty hours a week in a grocery store. There wasn't much spare time, but he escaped to wild country whenever possible.

During winter and spring vacations the destination of Mech and his friends was often New York's Adirondack State Park, a wild area as big as the state of Vermont. Although their stated goal was to trap furbearers, their catch was not as important as their adventures—snowshoeing many miles each day, observing the tracks and other signs of otters, beavers, deer, and other wildlife, and especially following the tracks of fishers, which are fox-size members of the weasel family.

Dave Mech's intense interest in wilderness led to an unusual summer job: live-trapping black bears in the Adirondack Mountains. As a

In New York's Adirondack Mountains, Dave Mech assisted in a study of black bears, which involved trapping and releasing both adult bears and cubs.

crew member of the Cornell University research project, he gained experience in trapping, anesthetizing, and handling bears. Bobcats and coyotes were sometimes captured, too. Dave Mech felt more certain than ever that he wanted to work with such animals. As he began his senior year at Cornell, he hoped to continue on to graduate school and to have a carnivore research project.

In Indiana, Dr. Durward Allen, Professor of Wildlife Ecology at Purdue University, had just such a project in mind: a study of the wolf-moose relationships on Isle Royale. Moose had been on the island since the early 1900s, and their population had undergone some severe ups and downs. Then, about 1949, wolves crossed on ice from Canada to the island. People began finding the remains of moose killed by wolves. A preliminary study by National Park Service biologist James Cole indicated that a person in a small airplane could follow wolf tracks in the snow, see wolves, and also locate dead moose.

Dr. Allen believed that Isle Royale was an extraordinary natural laboratory for study of the relationship between a carnivore and its prey. With the cooperation of the Park Service, he planned a series of studies and applied for funds from the National Science Foundation. Then he sought a special person to conduct the vital first stage of the project—someone with wilderness experience and a strong interest in carnivores. He found Dave Mech.

3 To See a Wolf

In June 1958, Dave Mech saw Isle Royale for the first time. With a group of biologists who were to advise him at the beginning of his project, he had boarded a National Park Service boat to take the seventy-mile trip to the island. After several hours Isle Royale appeared out of the haze—a forested ridge on the horizon, forty-five miles long. As the boat drew closer, Mech saw more details, including the island's rocky shore and dozens of smaller islands. "It was easy to imagine moose barging through the brush and wolves loping over the rocks," he recalls.

Mech lived part of the time at the summer headquarters of the National Park Service and part camping on the trail. He came to know the island very well, with all of its ridges, lakes, swamps, bays, coves, and points. Within a day of his arrival he saw the first moose of his life. Then he found a large footprint, like a dog's, in the mud of a trail—the track of a wolf.

His goal was to cover the hundred miles of trails as often as possible, collecting wolf scats in order to learn what the wolves ate in the summertime. He soon found that the scats were made up mostly of long, coarse moose hair, and sometimes of long, silky beaver hair. Mech also hoped to learn whether the wolves were concentrated in any one area, to find some of their kills, and to see a wolf.

There were some tourists and hikers on the island, but they seldom ventured far from the two visitor lodges. Few reached the island's inte-

On Isle Royale, Dave Mech observed moose and also hiked many times over the island's trails in search of wolf signs.

Isle Royale, largest island in Lake Superior, lies east of Minnesota's Superior National Forest, the region where Mech would later study wolves.

rior. Mech met only three groups of hikers there in the four summers of his study. In that period he walked 1,400 miles.

Park employees and commercial fishermen and their families also lived on Isle Royale in the summer. Some of them were skeptical about his study. Mech recalls, "I was told during my first week that there were six wolves on Isle Royale and that they were eating all the moose. What more was there to find out?"

He was also told that he was in some danger, traveling alone in wolf country. The Park Service advised him to carry a revolver. There were wolves around, no doubt. Their big footprints marked every trail and sandy beach. Some were quite fresh, perhaps made only minutes before Mech found them. Still, he saw no wolves. He sat atop high ridges and scanned open areas of the landscape with binoculars. He spent many hours watching. No wolves.

Dave Mech decided to lure wolves into view with bait. He buried some bones and meat on a beach where wolf tracks were common. The next day he found the bait dug up, and the tracks of a single wolf. Encouraged, Mech buried more bait and built a hiding place under a nearby spruce tree. In the evening he hid there and waited for the wolf to return.

Several hours passed. Nothing stirred. He watched the stars and listened to the swishing sound of waves on the beach. Suddenly the swishing turned to splashing. Something was coming toward him through the shallow water! Two forms loomed out of the darkness—a cow moose and its calf.

Moose were the only animals Mech ever saw while watching "wolf bait." He concentrated more and more on observing moose, especially to see how many calves the females had—an indication of the health of the entire moose population on the island. He also surveyed the aspen, birch, and other plants on which moose browse, to assess their food supply. At the end of each day, Dave Mech wrote detailed notes about his findings and experiences in a journal.

Late in the summer a work crew found the remains of a moose and

Between the parallel ridges of Isle Royale lie ponds, swamps, and lakes, which are vital habitat for the moose and beaver that wolves eat.

led Mech to it. Grasses and ferns were flattened where wolves had lain near their kill. Mech examined what they had left. The wolves had picked the bones clean and, in fact, many of the bones were missing. Mech couldn't find the skull but judged from the size of the other bones that the moose had been a calf. He also knew that he had to find and examine many, many wolf kills in order to learn more about the wolf-moose relationship, as Adolph Murie had learned about wolf predation on mountain sheep.

Though he never stopped looking for wolves, by the end of the summer Mech was resigned to examining moose bones, assessing moose food plants, gathering wolf scats, and watching moose, knowing that these activities were a vital part of his research. He left Isle Royale in late August with mixed feelings. He had spent nearly eight weeks in wolf country but had not seen or heard a wolf. But he would be back.

That fall Dave Mech began a new life—newly married to Betty

Ann Smith, whom he had met at Cornell, and newly enrolled as a graduate student at Purdue University. He studied his journals from the summer, analyzed the contents of the wolf scats he had collected, and conferred with Dr. Allen about the next stage of the project—aerial observation of wolves and moose in the wintertime.

Though wolves had been observed from the air before, the Isle Royale project was a pioneer study because Mech aimed to watch wolves for long periods as his aircraft circled. No one knew whether wolves would accept this, grow accustomed to the aircraft, and act naturally.

Mech returned to Isle Royale in February 1959 via ski-equipped airplane, the only way to reach the island in winter. There were only three people on the huge island: Mech, pilot Don Murray, and a park employee. Soon Mech and Murray were aloft in a two-seat, ski-equipped airplane that carried a two and one-half-hour fuel supply. They went looking for wolves.

Their search began along the island's perimeter, since wolves were reported to travel often on the ice there. The first step was to learn how to identify wolf tracks from the air. Mech saw what he thought were tracks of wolves and told Murray to follow them. The aircraft headed toward the northern end of the island, just three hundred feet in the air, as both biologist and pilot watched the snowy landscape below. Then they saw wolves—six of them—lying on a ridge. The wolves rose to their feet when the aircraft dropped to within two hundred feet, but they seemed more curious than frightened.

"A few miles away I saw nine other wolves," Mech recalls. "They chased after the plane when it came low near them. We had to leave in order to refuel. When we came back, all fifteen wolves were together. At last I could see the objects of my study, the animals I was so curious about. And when we found the same pack two days later, the wolves showed little interest in the airplane. My dream of watching wolves from the air seemed to be coming true."

Dave Mech's dream was threatened by a personal problem: airsickness. On nearly every flight he became ill as the airplane circled and banked sharply in order to find and stay near wolves. Preventive drugs helped very little. Only the experience of many hours of flying finally quelled his nausea.

Mech spent most of his flying time watching the main wolf pack. But he located other wolves—a pair and a pack of three. Much as he wanted to concentrate exclusively on wolves, he also spent many hours searching for moose, since it was vital to learn the numbers of prey animals upon which the wolves depended.

"Each time I spotted a moose, Don Murray dived the plane at it to make it run. Then any other unseen moose nearby also ran, and I could count them. This might sound like fun, but just thinking about it makes me airsick. We spent a total of forty-five hours doing this and found there were about six hundred moose on the island."

By flying every day that weather allowed, Mech gathered more and more information about the winter lives of wolves and moose. He learned the commonly used travel routes of the wolves. One day he decided to use this knowledge and finally get close to the wolves—on the ground.

"Don Murray and I were following the big pack. I realized that if they stayed on their usual route, they would file across the ice of a little cove fifty feet from an old fish house along the shore. We flew ahead of the pack, landed, then snowshoed as fast as we could to the fish house."

Their ambush worked. With the door cracked open just wide enough for a camera lens, they watched as each of the fifteen wolves strolled onto the ice. "We excitedly clicked pictures as the animals assembled in front of us. Then one individual wandered to within fifteen feet and stood broadside to us, calmly staring at the doorway. I snapped the camera, and the wolf cocked its head. It looked like a big friendly dog. It was easy to believe that I could have reached out and petted the wolf."

"Although my standing face-to-face with a wild wolf had little sci-

Close to wolves for the first time, Dave Mech watched through the fishhouse door as the pack approached on the ice.

entific value," Mech later wrote, "it certainly helped inspire me to learn all I could about the animal that had such a calm and gentle look yet earned its living by killing."

From the air Mech saw wolves hunting, rushing, chasing, and sometimes attacking moose. One of the first encounters occurred on March 1, 1959. After Mech and Murray found the big pack traveling near a lake, they left to refuel, then returned late in the day to find the wolves surrounding a large bull moose, which stood in a small grove of trees.

"He was bleeding steadily from the throat and had difficulty holding his head up. About one hundred fifty square feet of the surrounding snow was covered with blood. The animal's lower left hind leg was bloody, and he leaned against a tree, keeping his right hind leg centered under him.

"Most of the wolves were yards away, resting and playing, but a few were licking the bloody snow. One wolf in particular, whose legs were covered with blood, was harassing the moose. It stayed near the bull most of the time, often nipping at the injured leg. However, each time the moose faced it or any nearby wolves, they scrambled away. At 6:30 P.M. we left because of darkness."

Unfavorable weather kept Mech from returning for three days. Then he saw only bones scattered around the place where the moose had been. The pilot landed on the nearby lake and Mech snowshoed to the kill site. By examining the remains, he learned that the moose had been an old bull, at least eight years old.

From the air Mech also saw several moose successfully defend themselves against wolves. He wondered why they lived and others died. The only way to find out was to examine the dead ones. By continually locat-

By examining dead moose and learning something about their health before wolves killed them, Mech began to understand why some moose died while others survived.

ing the wolves, he spotted several of their kills, which he then tried to reach on foot. Although most of the meat and hide was usually gone, from the skull and bones Mech could learn the moose's sex, approximate age, and its general health. He carried a small saw and cut through a leg bone to see the color of the marrow. This revealed the amount of fat in the marrow—a good indicator of the animal's health (the greater the reserve of fat in winter, the better).

Each dead moose was a treasure to Dave Mech's study. He felt encouraged when he returned to Purdue in mid-March. His aerial spying was beginning to reveal a picture of the wolf-moose relationship on Isle Royale.

4 Further Adventures on Isle Royale

Dave Mech spent part of two more winters and three summers on Isle Royale. In the summertime he was joined by his wife, Betty Ann, and they lived in a cabin on one of the small islands near Isle Royale. He commuted to work by boat and continued to hike the trails, collect scats, watch moose, and learn more about the summer lives of predator and prey.

In 1959, he caught brief glimpses of wolves. One June day Mech was on the Greenstone Ridge trail when he found fresh wolf tracks. Then he heard what seemed to be whimpering and whining several yards behind him. He wheeled around but saw nothing. He hid in the brush and waited, but there were no further sounds.

Mech began hiking again. About two miles farther along he suddenly saw a wolf standing in the trail just fifty feet ahead. They looked at one another for about ten seconds; then the wolf disappeared into the brush. Mech ran to the place but could neither see nor hear the wolf. This animal and two others met briefly that summer were the only ones Mech saw during his 4,400 miles of walking on Isle Royale.

In forested regions, wolves can easily avoid being seen by people. They are easier to observe in the open tundra of the Arctic, where, in some areas, they are also less fearful of humans. Studies of such predators as lions and cheetahs in African game parks have been relatively

easy because of the open terrain and the animals' acceptance of people watching them from vehicles. Where visibility is poor, a scientist may have to use bait or wait patiently near a den in order to gradually win the wild animals' trust. Dave Mech learned that the wolves of Isle Royale were too wary for this kind of close-up observation.

In the summer of 1960, Dave Mech had a terrible scare, but not from a wolf. On the trail again, he was carrying a forty-pound backpack that included photographic gear, food, and camping equipment. He intended to spend the night in a lean-to along the trail. He was already far from his boat when he squatted to tie a shoelace. Suddenly he felt a sharp pain in his back. He couldn't straighten up. He managed to cut a walking stick and carried the pack two and one-half miles to a wooden shelter, where it would be safe for a few days. He struggled the remaining six miles to his boat and then raced twenty-five miles around the island to reach Betty Ann at the cabin.

As it turned out, this speed was vital because the back injury affected his leg muscles and he was soon immobile. He feared that his wolf studies might be at an end. Betty Ann consulted with medical experts in Michigan by telephone, however, and learned that the injury would probably mend if he rested for several days. This proved to be true. After this incident Mech was more careful in lifting and carrying heavy weights. He suffered one recurrence in the winter of 1961 when he tripped while snowshoeing, and was again bedridden, but he resumed work after about ten days.

Early in 1960 Dave Mech for the first time saw wolves actually kill a moose. He and pilot Murray had followed the main pack much of the day. About 4:00 P.M. they left the wolves crossing a lake while they went to refuel the airplane once more. Upon their return the men saw the wolves running on an open ridge toward a cow moose and two calves. (By wintertime a moose calf is a large animal, weighing at least three

---

Mech hiked 4,400 miles on the island but saw only three wolves. Usually, the wary mammals could hide easily in lush summer vegetation.

hundred pounds, though not as big as an eight-hundred-pound cow or a one-thousand-pound bull.) From the way the wolves had veered direction about one and one-half miles from the moose, it appeared that they had smelled their prey at that distance. The first of the wolves caught up with the fleeing moose, and here is how Mech described the action that followed:

"The cow was immediately behind the calves, and twice she feinted toward the wolves, which leaped out of the way. Most of the pack began catching up, and as the moose entered a small cedar swamp (the nearest conifer cover), four or five animals tore at the rump and sides of a calf and clung to it. Within fifty feet, the calf went down in a thick clump of cedars. The cow and the other calf continued through the cover with two wolves still following for twenty yards. When these wolves gave up, the moose stopped and returned fifty yards toward the wounded calf. Gradually, however, the moose drifted back toward where they originally had started. Most of the wolves concentrated on the wounded calf, which remained where it had fallen. The cedars obscured our vision, but the calf appeared dead within five minutes after it fell."

Mech wanted to examine a dead moose before it was consumed, yet he wasn't sure whether he should try. Opinions varied about whether wolves were dangerous to humans. Meeting a wolf on a trail was one thing; chasing fifteen wolves away from their food was another. Don Murray felt that Mech would be in great danger and urged him not to try. Mech decided to take the risk.

After the aircraft skied to a stop on a nearby lake, Mech made sure his revolver was in his backpack. Murray said he would "buzz" low over the wolves if they seemed to threaten Mech. Then he took off to watch overhead. Mech began snowshoeing toward the place where the moose calf had fallen.

"It took me half an hour to snowshoe to the kill," Mech said. "According to the pilot, most of the wolves ran off when I was within one hundred fifty yards. I had a movie camera and hoped to sneak up and take some films of wolves at the kill, but as I came closer I saw

In the wintertime, wolves often travel on the ice and hard-packed snow of lakes and streams, where traveling is usually easier than on land.

several wolves run off—too far away for filming. When I was about seventy-five feet away I saw two wolves still at the carcass. They lifted their bloodied faces, saw me, and glided off quickly."

Mech spent the next forty-five minutes examining and photographing the carcass. He saw no wolves but heard the pack howling. The wolves had gathered on a ridge about two hundred fifty yards away, and Murray kept circling above them.

Dave Mech was right at the carcass, inspecting some of the moose's internal organs, when he noticed a change in the sound of the airplane. It was roaring down and zooming up, flying toward him in a series of dives. This was Murray's prearranged signal. The wolves were coming.

"I looked up and saw two big wolves running toward me. They were probably a hundred feet away. The movie camera was in my hand. Should I take pictures or reach for the revolver? I chose the revolver.

"The instant the wolves saw me move they stopped, turned, and fled more quickly than they had come. Of course, it wasn't because they saw the gun. I think they just couldn't smell me through all the odor of the freshly killed moose, so they thought I was gone. Don Murray told me later that two wolves seemed to playfully race one another back to the moose. Only when they saw me move did they realize I was still there."

This showed Mech more than ever that wolves are extremely afraid of humans. He stopped carrying the revolver. It was an extra weight, and he figured that carrying a loaded gun was probably more dangerous than any wolf he would meet. Eventually Mech concluded that "there is no basis for the belief that healthy, wild wolves in North America are of any danger to human beings." Biologists who study lions, tigers, and most other large predators come to a similar conclusion. Their greatest risk of injury or death comes not from wild animals but from vehicle or airplane accidents.

Mech and Murray were a good team, though their attitudes about wolves were at first very different. Don Murray was a veteran wolf hunter and had strong antiwolf feelings. But after watching them for many hours he began to respect and like them. He saw wolves travel fifteen to twenty miles a day, feed on old carcasses, make many unsuccessful attempts at killing moose, and still rush playfully about in temperatures of 20° F below zero.

Still, some of his old feelings returned when he saw a pack swarming over a moose calf; he usually rooted for the moose. One afternoon, however, the men trailed the main wolf pack as it came upon nineteen different moose, yet failed to kill one. Don Murray felt sorry for them. "I hope they get one tonight," he said.

Eventually both men came to share the same attitude: This is the way nature works; let's watch it, describe it, and try to understand it; who are we to judge it?

Further Adventures on Isle Royale   25

They expected to watch the main pack for parts of three winters, but that plan was unexpectedly thrown into doubt on March 1, 1960. That day they located the big pack traveling on the ice of a harbor. The wolves reached the northeast tip of Isle Royale, then kept heading north—toward Canada, some twenty miles away. Their ancestors, long ago, had reached the island by crossing the ice, and it appeared that the wolves were now intent upon leaving. The single file of wolves traveled a half mile . . . a mile . . . a mile and a half . . . *away* from Isle Royale.

As Mech watched from the airplane, this moose stood its ground against the big wolf pack. After a few minutes the wolves left and hunted for easier prey.

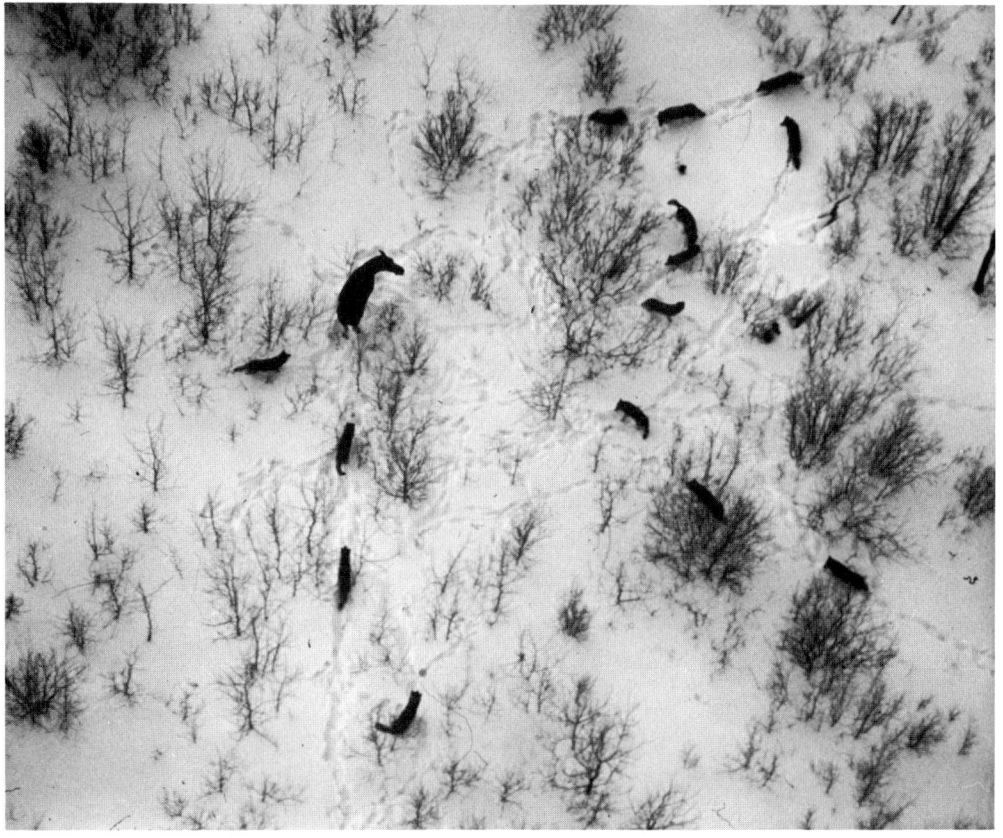

Then some pack members began to hesitate and stop. The leader seemed determined to keep going. Several times it returned to the others and seemed to urge them on.

Watching this conflict, Dave Mech felt some mixed emotions, too. Should he continue to simply observe the wolves, interfering in their lives as little as possible, even if the main subject of his study was about to leave? Or should he tell Don Murray to dive the airplane at the wolves and drive them back to Isle Royale?

Fortunately, Mech did not have to make this choice. After traveling another half mile, the wolves reached a section of rough, jagged ice. All of the pack members sat down, except for the leader. It urged the others on, without success. The lead wolf then took the pack back to Isle Royale, and Dave Mech sighed in relief.

By the end of this third winter study period, Mech had spent about seventy hours watching the big wolf pack from his aerial observation post. He had observed wolves traveling, mating, playing, sleeping, hunting, and killing. Some of his observations were too limited to have much meaning. But his many sightings of wolves hunting moose showed that wolves are not the all-powerful killers that people imagine them to be. Although he saw several moose killed by wolves, time after time he observed moose escape unharmed. Usually a moose survived just by standing its ground. The wolves tried for a short time to force it to run, then left. Wolves were even reluctant to attack a wounded moose that stood at bay. Mech saw a moose beat two wolves into the snow with its hooves, and another brush off a biting wolf against a tree. Other biologists have reported moose killing wolves.

Moose that ran were more vulnerable to attack. However, most of the moose that ran and were chased by wolves usually escaped, either by outdistancing or outlasting their pursuers. "In one day the big pack chased fifteen moose without catching a single one," Mech recalls. "Altogether, I saw this pack try to kill seventy-seven moose, but all they got was six."

Although wolves wounded this moose when it fled, it stopped running and successfully defended itself. The next day the wolf pack had killed another moose, sixteen miles away.

Of the fifty-one wolf-killed moose he examined, Mech found none in the prime of life, between one and six years of age. Most were calves or were older than ten years. Many were infested with ticks, had tapeworm cysts in their lungs, or had infected, swollen jawbones. Thus the wolves killed the weak, diseased moose and were seldom able to kill strong, healthy moose. Although the big pack killed a moose every three or four days, their predation was not depleting the moose population, which produced more than two hundred calves each year. Many female moose had twin calves—a sign of reproductive health in moose.

Dave Mech concluded that the wolves and moose of Isle Royale had reached a sort of balance in their populations. He was surprised to find that the wolves were not reproducing. He had seen wolves mating during their breeding season of late January to early March, but there was no sign that pups had been born. A single pup was born in 1962, the year after Mech completed his study. He wondered how and why the wolves kept their numbers in check.

In the summer of 1961, Dave Mech helped another graduate student, Philip Shelton, who was to continue the Isle Royale study. Mech could look back on some extraordinary adventures and solid accomplishments as he wrote his thesis for a Doctor of Philosophy (Ph.D.) degree. He had learned a great deal about the wolves of Isle Royale. But he also knew how little of their lives he really understood, and his curiosity about wolves was aroused more than ever.

5 Thunder and Lightning

A long, mournful howl sounded in the evening quiet. It was a young wolf, trying out its voice. The wolf was answered by another howl, from Dave Mech, for the wolf lived in the backyard of the Mech home in Minnesota.

After his experiences on Isle Royale, it was probably inevitable that Dave Mech would settle in Minnesota—the only state other than Alaska with a large population of wolves. Now called Dr. Mech, he did postdoctoral studies and became a research associate at the University of Minnesota, and later he taught and was a research ecologist at Macalester College. Mech did some preliminary studies of the wolves in northeastern Minnesota but was unable to get the financial backing needed for a long-term project. For a time Mech worked on the development and testing of equipment used to track wildlife by radio signals. He also wrote *The Wolves of Isle Royale,* which became a popular book in a series published about the fauna of the national parks.

During 1967 Dave and Betty Ann Mech went through a particularly trying time. By then they had four children—Sharon, Stephen, Christopher, and Nicholas—and lived in a house in the suburbs of Minneapolis. Mech had no formal job and was writing a long, authoritative book about wolves. It was a difficult time, with little income and no certainty about what lay ahead when the book was finished. There were

As the wolf pups grew older, Dave Mech observed changes in their behavior with each other, with dogs, and with people.

job opportunities, but they meant leaving Minnesota or studying such animals as pheasants. Dave Mech clung to his dream of studying wolves in the north country.

Then Mech received a call from the director of the Como Zoo in St. Paul, Minnesota. A wolf there had given birth to several pups. Would he like to have one or two? Mech knew that raising wolf pups would

30

add to the stress on himself and his family. But he also believed that actually raising wolf pups would give him knowledge about the early physical development and behavior of wolves that he couldn't get any other way. Thus, in May 1967, two wolf pups came to live with the Mech family.

"The first things we needed were baby bottles, for the pups were still nursing from their mother. They were only ten days old. About all they could do was whine, move their heads from side to side, and suck strongly on a nipple. They could neither see nor hear."

The Mechs decided to name the male Thunder and the female Lightning. The pups developed rapidly. At three weeks, they each consumed a pint of milk daily and were able to walk and growl. Soon they were running, playing, and chewing on shoes and other objects with their brand-new teeth.

"Our children, ages three to seven, had completely fallen in love with them, and our dog had adopted them as if they were her own," Mech recalled. "It looked as though we were going to have one big happy pack. Then, suddenly, a strange thing happened. At twenty-seven days of age, Thunder and Lightning began fighting."

It was very serious fighting, not play. Mech usually stopped the fights by separating the pups. One time he let them continue, to see what would happen. They growled, wrestled, and bit for minute after minute. The fur on their backs became ragged from chewing and Lightning began to bleed. Mech separated them for the night. During the next two days the Mechs had more trouble keeping the wolves from fighting, so they decided to return one pup to the zoo. The pups were taken outdoors and brought together for one last time so that their photographs could be taken.

"Thunder and Lightning rushed to each other and began fighting in their usual way. But this time something unusual happened. When Thunder pressed Lightning to the ground she did not fight back. Instead she rolled over on her back and whined. At the same time, Thunder stopped his attack and stood stiffly over her with his tail straight up in the air. Suddenly I knew what had happened. The pups had finally decided which one was boss."

From that day on Thunder was the dominant, or alpha, wolf and Lightning the subordinate one. They fought no more. Among groups of wild or captive wolves, every individual soon learns its rank in the group, so very little fighting occurs. A wolf pack is usually led by a mated pair—the alpha male and the alpha female. If the pups had been part of a wolf pack, with adults around, their order of dominance probably would have been worked out more easily.

With their social status decided, Thunder and Lightning played, explored, and rested together. They especially enjoyed attacking a cardboard box or an old rag, ripping it apart with their teeth. One day Dave Mech put on some old clothes and wrestled with Thunder and Lightning. "They grabbed and tugged at my clothing and began peeling shreds of it off me. This reminded me very much of scenes I had seen in the wild where a pack of wolves had pulled a moose down and were tugging and ripping at it.

"That's when I realized what these games were. In the wild, this kind of play would have helped the pups practice the patterns that they would use in killing and eating their prey. Instead of peeling cardboard boxes, they would be stripping fur or feathers off dead animals that their parents brought them."

Although the wolf pups had been given the usual shots against canine diseases, Thunder fell ill and died of distemper at the age of three and one-half months. Lightning was sick, too, but survived. She grew rapidly and looked more and more like an adult wolf. At the age of five months her behavior changed markedly. Until then she had been friendly to any person or dog who entered the backyard where she lived. Then she became afraid of strangers and threatened some strange dogs.

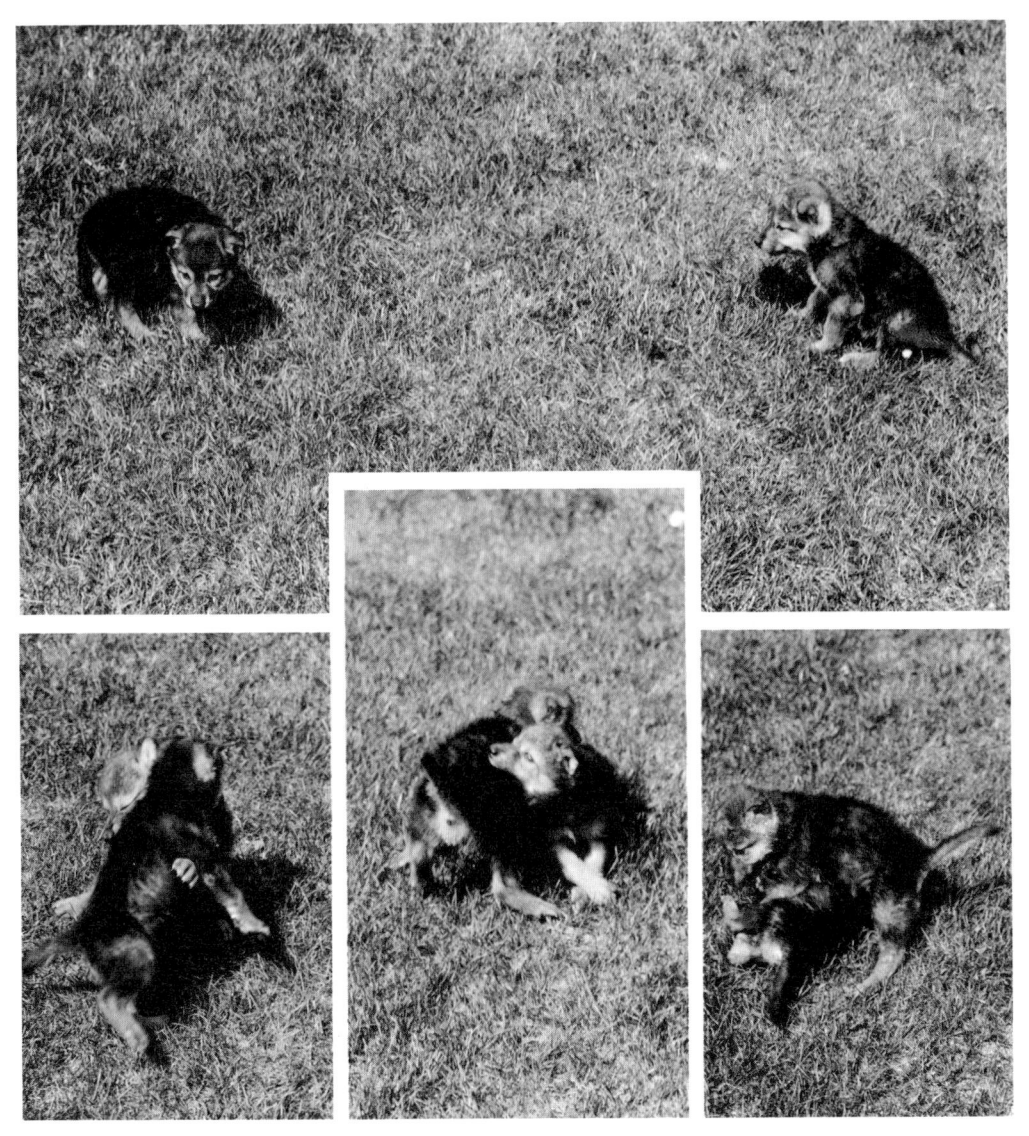

Set on a lawn to be photographed when thirty days old, Thunder and Lightning soon rushed toward each other. They fought, growled, and tried to bite each other's back. Then Lightning rolled over, whining, and Thunder raised his tail. From then on he was the dominant, or alpha, wolf.

She remained as friendly as ever with people and dogs she knew, however.

Dave Mech suspected that wild wolves may follow the same behavior pattern. Wild wolf pups form social ties with members of their own pack during their first few months of life. By the time they travel widely enough to meet strange wolves, however, they no longer make social ties easily. Instead, they become unfriendly or fearful toward the strangers. "This is probably what keeps each pack separate from others in the wild," Mech said. "If pups were to attach emotionally to alien wolves, the unity of their pack would break down, and so would the entire organization of wolf society. By staying apart, each group of wolves can hunt for food in a different area and find enough to eat."

Lightning was gentle and affectionate with her "pack" of people and dogs. She greeted people the way a subordinate wolf greets a dominant wolf—by excitedly nipping and licking its mouth. Some mornings Lightning bounded onto Dave Mech's bed and awakened him that way.

She swam in a nearby creek with the Mech children and was well liked in the neighborhood. The trouble was, Lightning was not supposed to be out in the neighborhood. Mech had built a tall fence around the large backyard where Lightning stayed, and she was usually attached by a chain to an overhead wire so that she could roam all over the yard. Still, she managed to escape occasionally. Usually she was found by the Mechs and brought home within a few hours. But Dave Mech worried that some incident might occur in which Lightning would be blamed—rightly or not—for harming or simply scaring someone. This, he knew, would stir up the old hatred and fear of wolves in some people.

Lightning's escapades troubled Dave Mech in another way, too. When he saw her running free in the wooded valley behind the house, he felt she belonged there, not on a chain. Yet, turning Lightning loose in a wild area was no solution. She would be rejected and perhaps attacked by other wolves and would know little about getting her own food.

The Mech family was Lightning's "pack." Here she gives "pack" member Betty Ann Mech a wolf greeting—nipping and licking at her mouth.

On a rainy night in April 1968, Lightning escaped once more. She roamed the neighborhood for half the night. "When she returned and I fastened her to the chain that held her to an artificial life, she was a different animal," Mech recalls. "She began to struggle fiercely to escape. She was still tame and gentle with me, but she finally had a taste of what it was like to act as her heritage had dictated—to be wild and free. As I watched Lightning straining desperately at her chain, pacing, whining, and jumping frantically, I suddenly realized how very wrong it is to try to tame a wolf.

"The next morning she was her old self. But I wasn't mine. I had seen what I had known all along—that wolves weren't made for backyards and people. They were made for other wolves and for vast expanses of wilderness."

Though the wolf is the ancestor of all pet dogs, many attempts to make pets of them end in tragedy. Some pet wolves have run off for a romp in the woods and were shot dead. One pair of wolves, used in a school assembly program that toured the United States, was slipped some poison in New York City. And Lois Crisler, who raised wolves in Alaska and described her experiences in the book *Arctic Wild,* eventually killed them because she couldn't stand to see what captivity had done to them. These sad stories can be multiplied many times for other wild animals kept as pets.

Mech knew that Lightning would have to be a captive as long as she lived, but he felt that he could no longer bear to be her captor. He took her to the zoo from which she had come and said that he would rather have her dead than confined in a cage the rest of her life. If she wasn't killed, he urged that she be given a home in another zoo with a large area for her to run, preferably where he would never see her again.

From Lightning and Thunder, Dave Mech learned things about wolves that he could never have observed in the wild. He was grateful for that. He also knew that he might someday raise wolves in cages for research purposes. But Lightning had been much more than a research animal. She had been a member of the Mech family and was now separated forever from her pack.

Mech's book *The Wolf: The Ecology and Behavior of an Endangered Species* was published in 1970. In his review, the late Supreme Court Justice William O. Douglas wrote, "This book will be our classic on the wolf." He was right. Of the book's many thousands of readers, only a few know the story of Lightning and understand the last words of Dave Mech's preface: "And lastly, to Lightning—if it is permissible to address a wolf in print—the only thing I can say is, 'I'm sorry.'"

6 Radio Tracking and Wolf Number 2407

Northern Minnesota is the home of the largest population of wolves in the United States outside of Alaska. They are most abundant in the Superior National Forest and its Boundary Waters Canoe Area, which together cover 1.5 million acres of forests, laced with rivers and sprinkled with hundreds of lakes.

For several years, whenever he could arrange it, Dave Mech explored this vast wilderness. Moose were present but deer were more abundant and were the main prey of the wolves. Just by snowshoeing along the lake shores in the wintertime, Mech found the remains of wolf-killed deer. From the air he saw wolves, followed them, and located more of the deer they had killed. The information he could get this way was limited, however. There were many packs of wolves, not just one main pack as on Isle Royale. It was not possible to follow one pack from day to day because he could not easily tell one pack from another. Nor could he usually see wolves unless they were in the open in the wintertime, visible on the snow of a frozen lake or river.

The wolves were there, but Mech needed to locate them quickly and to identify specific packs. Only then could he follow the fortunes of individual wolves and packs and investigate how wolves were spaced in their populations. The solution to this problem, he suspected, lay in radio

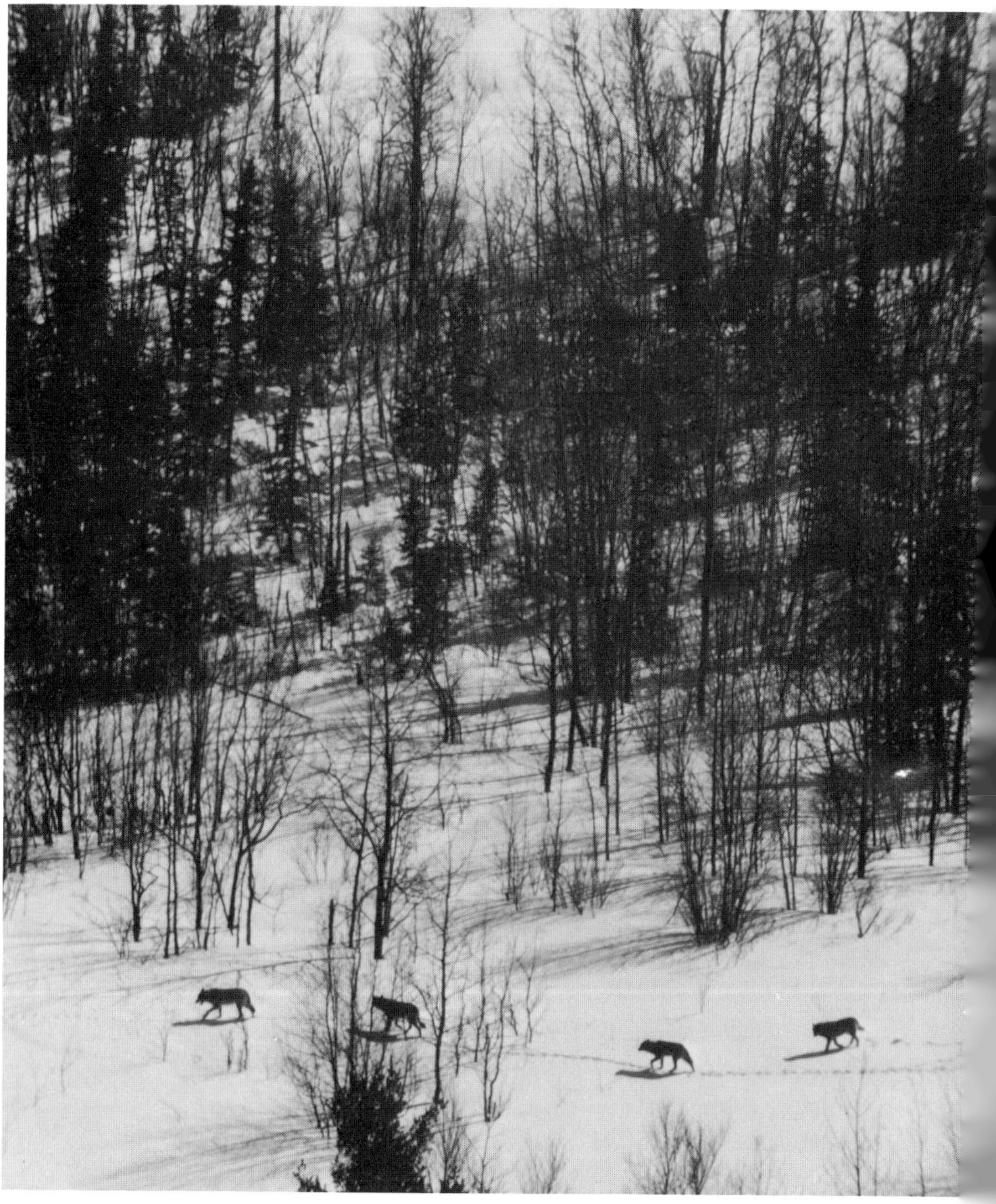

tracking. In 1968, Mech obtained enough research funds to start a small-scale radio tracking study of wolves in Minnesota.

The technique of putting radio transmitters on wild animals in order to study them was developed in the early 1960s. It has since been used successfully on many species, from leopards to vampire bats. The first step is to capture the animals. Each species has special characteristics that affect how, and how easily, this is done. Black bears, for example, can usually be lured by bait into large box-type traps. Mountain lions can be trailed and treed by dogs and can then be injected with an immobilizing drug from a rifle-fired dart.

Wolves, however, can outrun most dogs and are too wary to enter box traps. The only way to catch wolves, Mech found, was to use special steel leg-hold traps, which hold a wolf but do little harm to its large, strong feet. At first Mech set traps for wolves in the late fall and winter, but two animals suffered from frozen toes while in traps overnight. From then on he trapped wolves only in warmer months, from May to October.

To outwit a wolf and induce it to step into a trap is not easy. "This has been the greatest challenge in the entire project," Mech says. "There were times in the first few years when I came close to giving up because we had such difficulty catching wolves."

Each captured wolf is a great prize, not as a trophy, but as a living animal that returns to its pack and resumes its normal life in the wild. The first step is to learn as much as possible about the captured wolf. To accomplish this, the wolf is injected with a drug that makes it unconscious. (This is easily done, as captured wolves are usually meek and docile.) Then numbered identification tags are put in its ears, and information about the wolf's sex, size, weight, and breeding condition is recorded. A blood sample is also taken and later analyzed in a labora-

---

In 1968, Dave Mech began to study wolves and their main prey, deer, in the vast wild lands of northern Minnesota.

A tough collar containing a radio transmitter and batteries is put around the neck of each captured wolf. Back in the wild, each wolf can be located by its distinctive radio signal.

tory. Finally, a collar containing a battery-powered radio transmitter is put around the wolf's neck.

The collar package has to be made of tough material if the radio is to send signals for two years, the maximum life of the batteries. In the wild the collar and its contents are subjected to deep-freezing temperatures, to rain and snow, to bumps and scrapes as the wolf travels, and sometimes to biting or chewing by the wolf's packmates. Molded acrylic plastic or other strong materials help most of the radios endure this trial.

Dave Mech or an assistant stay near the wolf until the animal recovers from the drug, gets up, and runs away. Each radio transmits signals at a different frequency, so each wolf is "tagged" with a distinctive signal. As long as the wolf's transmitter works, the animal's location can be detected by directional antennas mounted on ground vehicles or aircraft. From an airplane at an altitude of 1,500 feet, a wolf's signal can be detected ten to fifteen miles away.

With practice, a person in an airplane can use radio tracking to get much closer—just a few hundred feet above a wolf. In the wintertime this is usually close enough to see the wolves' bodies against the snow, as well as to record their activities—resting, sleeping, traveling, hunting, or feeding—and to scan the area for the remains of a kill. Catching sight of wolves in the summertime is more difficult.

Five wolves were radio-tagged in the fall and winter of 1968–69. To Dave Mech's surprise, only two were members of packs. The others were lone wolves—animals that were not part of a pack, either temporarily or permanently. Some lone wolves seem to be social outcasts of a pack. They trail behind it and feed on scraps the others leave. Other lone wolves avoid all contact with packs and make a living completely on their own. Sometimes a male and female lone wolf meet, mate, and try to form their own pack. Most lone wolves, Dave Mech found, are "doomed to a nomadic life of trying to avoid packs."

Though initially he had just five wolves to work with, Dave Mech soon gained some useful information about their movements, behavior, and ecology. One radio-collared wolf was part of a pack of five. After finding these wolves many times over a span of several months and marking their locations on a map, Mech found that the pack used a range of forty-three square miles. Twice he saw the pack chase alien wolves out of its home range. This was evidence that a pack of wolves defends a territory—something that wolfmen had long wondered about.

Mech also began to learn about the wolf-deer relationship in Minnesota. He saw wolves chasing deer. In one case the deer were in snow up to their bellies and had some difficulty bounding. But a pursuing wolf had even greater trouble and lay down to rest after a chase of about two hundred fifty yards. The deer stopped and alertly watched their backtrail for several minutes until they were sure the wolf had given up.

Another time, a single wolf pursued a deer almost four miles. The snow was not as deep. At the end of the chase, both deer and wolf were so tired that the deer had slowed to a fast walk and the wolf to a trot. When the wolf closed the gap between them, the deer went down quickly. Dave Mech inspected its remains and found that the deer had

Little food goes to waste when wolves succeed in killing prey. After a pack leaves, a lone wolf may approach cautiously and eat the remaining scraps.

arthritis in one hind foot—a defect that may have affected its running ability and one that the wolf may have been able to detect by seeing the deer's gait.

In the first year of his radio-tracking studies, Dave Mech also began to learn more about the traveling ability of wolves. On Isle Royale he had seen the main pack cover as much as forty-five miles in one day. None of the five wolves Mech followed traveled nearly that much, but over a two-month period one lone wolf, called number 1051, traveled about five hundred miles. Once during 1051's travels, Mech saw the wolf being chased by several loggers with axes. The wolf escaped. Number 1051 was last seen in late April 1969, about one hundred twenty-two miles in a straight line from where he had started. Though Mech searched widely for signals from 1051, the animal was never found again. He may have traveled beyond the range of aircraft, or his radio may have stopped transmitting.

Another wolf disappeared into Canada. Mech searched for her signal in a radius of thirty-five miles from her last location but failed to find her. By late summer of 1969, only two of the five radio-tagged wolves could be found. A few months later one of these wolves was killed by a trapper, who notified Mech. He examined her uterus and found that she had borne five pups during the summer.

The success of his initial radio-tracking study encouraged such organizations as the New York Zoological Society to give more research funds to Mech. Eight wolves were captured and radio-tagged in the fall of 1969, and two more the following spring. From an airplane Mech discovered a wolf den where several pups were raised in the summer of 1970. He chose not to disturb the den.

That same summer he became a full-time wildlife research biologist for the United States Fish and Wildlife Service, with the responsibility of carrying out research on rare and endangered carnivores in the Midwest. Study of the wolf would be emphasized. With funds from government agencies and scientific and conservation organizations, and a stable, long-term study under way, Mech was able to assemble a research staff of technicians, graduate students, student interns, and volunteer students. This enabled him to broaden the wolf project, to begin investigations he previously had no time for. It also meant that he had many scientific reports to write about his findings and less time in the wild outdoors. This sacrifice seemed worthwhile, though, as he planned expanded research on the wolf.

A basic goal, Dave Mech knew, was radio-tagging greater numbers of wolves. Inevitably some of them would be killed and some radios would fail, so the greater the number of wolves radio-tagged, the greater the chance of learning about the lives and movements of several packs. All sorts of information about wolves could be learned from radio tracking, but such research was especially suited to learning whether wolves had territories, and if so, how they maintained and defended them. Observations of one or two packs for a few years might not reveal much about these questions. Much more could be learned by observing several adjoining packs over the span of many years. This was Dave Mech's prime goal during the 1970s.

In the fall of 1970, Mech had fifteen wolves radio-tagged. Since then the numbers have varied, dwindling to a few, rising again as a result of autumn trapping success. At times, more than thirty wolves have been equipped with active radio transmitters, enabling Mech and his assistants to locate and observe eight adjoining wolf packs.

The toll on individual radio-tagged wolves has been heavy. Some were killed by cars, or by natural causes, including other wolves. Some were killed by people, though wolves have been legally protected since 1974 by the Federal Endangered Species Act. And some wolves survived, but their radios ceased signaling and they were not recaptured to be fitted with another. Only by catching and radio-tagging other members of packs (sometimes several at a time) has Dave Mech been able to continue to gather data on specific packs.

Wolves are intelligent and wary. Capturing and later recapturing wolves to fit them with radio collars has been a great challenge for Mech and his research team.

There is, however, one exception to this sad and frustrating record of dead wolves and dead radios: wolf number 2407. She was first trapped in the fall of 1971. Soon, her radio signals were enabling Dave Mech to locate her pack, called the Harris Lake Pack, of which she was the dominant, or alpha, female. At that time she was at least a year and a half old. She was captured again before her radio expired, and it was replaced. By the time 2407's radio needed replacing again, Dave Mech had followed her pack for three years and knew that its range was close to his headquarters in the Superior National Forest. Therefore it was convenient to deliberately try to recapture 2407—convenient but not necessarily easy. "It is always more difficult to catch a specific wolf than it is to catch just any wolf," Mech says. "Catching an experienced, trap-shy wolf is even harder, but we succeeded."

This set 2407 apart from all the other wolves because she was the one on which Dave Mech had the most data. Additional information about her life would be more valuable than that from a newly tagged wolf. "From that point on we made special efforts to recapture her before her radio would fail—every one or two years. In 1977, her radio failed prematurely and she was 'off the air' for almost a year. But one of her pups had been radio-tagged, so we were able to find the pack through his signal. And we could tell that 2407 was still in the pack because she was recognizable, by her radio collar, from the air."

When 2407 was caught in 1978, she was equipped with a special collar bearing two independent radios. One was designed to last longer than the other, but it soon failed. In the summer of 1979, Dave Mech and his assistants made a major effort to catch the wolf while her other radio still worked. Ordinarily it takes one or two hundred trap nights to catch a wolf. (A trap night is one trap set for a night; a hundred trap nights can be any combination of traps and nights, such as ten traps set for ten nights.) That summer their trapping effort totaled about five thousand trap nights. They caught several wolves, but not 2407. Fortunately, her radio kept working into 1980. In the summer of 1980,

Dave Mech's chief field assistant left and his replacement hadn't yet learned how to catch wolves. Mech himself did most of the trapping.

"This was fine with me," Mech said, "because at the time I wanted to spend more time on the project, rather than at my office. I put out about forty traps. We caught 2407's new mate. She's outlived at least two others. Then, after about three thousand trap nights, we caught her. On August 18 she was captured in a trap I had set in mid-June.

"I remember coming to my office in St. Paul, and my secretary's handing me a message from my field technician at the Superior National Forest, saying that they had caught 2407. I still have that note pinned on my wall.

"With less trouble we recaptured her in August of 1982 and gave her a radio collar with regular batteries, plus a solar energy cell, for insurance. We may never need to catch her again. She was then at least twelve years old; captive wolves have lived to be at least sixteen years old. Old 2407 is a real survivor, but there's always the chance that she may be killed. When she was caught in 1980 she had a fox snare around her neck; she had been caught by a trapper but tore loose."

This extraordinary wolf and her pack face a danger potentially more devastating than mere snares and guns. The territory of the Harris Lake Pack lies atop deposits of copper and nickel. An open pit mine has been proposed. If approved by the United States Forest Service and put in full operation, mining activity would destroy the land where 2407 has ranged all of her life and where generations of her descendants would normally live long after she dies. Laws against killing wolves or any other kind of wild animal are no guarantee that they will survive. A ruined habitat is usually as deadly as a bullet.

7 Exploring Wolf Territories

During thousands of hours of aerial observations, Dave Mech and his assistants have had some extraordinary glimpses of wolf behavior and ecology. They have seen hundreds of encounters between wolves and deer. They've watched wolves playing a sort of "tag" game with ravens, and wolves swimming across rivers. They've also seen wolf pups by their dens, or at grassy rendezvous sites where the pups live after they are big enough to leave their den but too small to go hunting.

Many biologists would leap at the chance to visit and observe a wolf den, but Dave Mech avoids them. "Early in this project," Mech said, "I decided that some of the great unanswered questions about wolves involved their populations. So I didn't want to affect the population here in any way. Visiting dens and perhaps causing wolves to move their pups might lead to the death of some pups. So I ruled out disturbing dens."

As radio tracking enabled Mech to locate wolf packs week after week and month after month, he marked the locations on a map. It became clear that the packs had well-defined territories, with little overlap. During a seven-year period, for example, 2407's pack varied in number from two to nine wolves, yet it still maintained the same general boundaries with neighboring packs.

Under normal conditions, a wolf pack seldom enters alien territory,

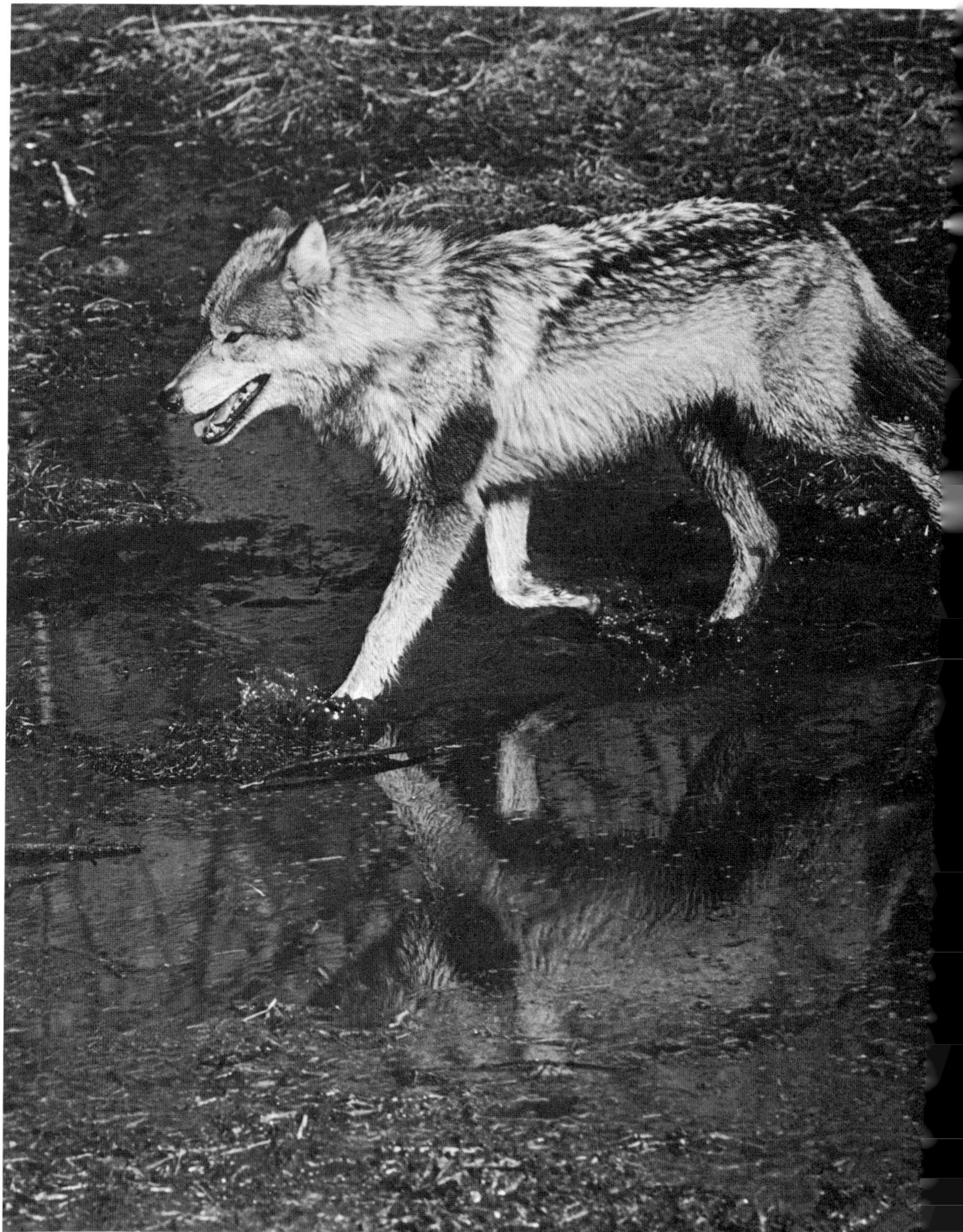

even if chasing prey. One observation of wolf tracks in the snow showed this dramatically. A pack called the Birch Lake Pack wounded a deer and chased it across a frozen river. Normally the wolves would have pursued it eagerly. The river, however, was on the border between their territory and that of the Harris Lake Pack. The Birch Lake Pack gave up and returned to its territory. On the following day the other pack found and ate the deer.

Before giving up the chase, though, the members of the Birch Lake Pack left scent marks of urine in the snow. To the casual onlooker, this may not have seemed remarkable—just routine wolf or dog behavior. But Dave Mech suspected, from other studies as well as his own, that scent marking plays an important role in maintaining wolf territories.

In the winter of 1971–72, he assigned two student interns to begin an investigation of wolf scent marking. On foot they followed the trails of wolf packs and noted the frequency and location of scent marks. During the following two winters, a graduate student named Roger Peters was the main investigator, along with Dave Mech.

By watching wolves in zoos, they learned that only mature, dominant wolves—mainly the alpha male and alpha female—urinate with a raised leg. Only a little urine is released each time. Although any urine mark or scat left by a wolf contains scents that have meanings to other wolves, the marks made with a raised leg are most important. In the wild, wolves leave this kind of scent mark on protruding, conspicuous objects (trees, rocks, snowbanks) along their regular travel routes (game paths, old logging trails, dirt roads, shores of frozen lakes). Scent marks are most abundant at junctions along these routes and at the edges of wolf territories.

"Roger Peters and I concluded that entire wolf territories are—you might say—sprinkled with scent marks," Mech explained. "Wherever a wolf travels, within a few minutes it will encounter a scent mark and

---

Wolves can trot for many miles, day or night, but do not wander aimlessly. Each wolf pack travels throughout a well-defined territory.

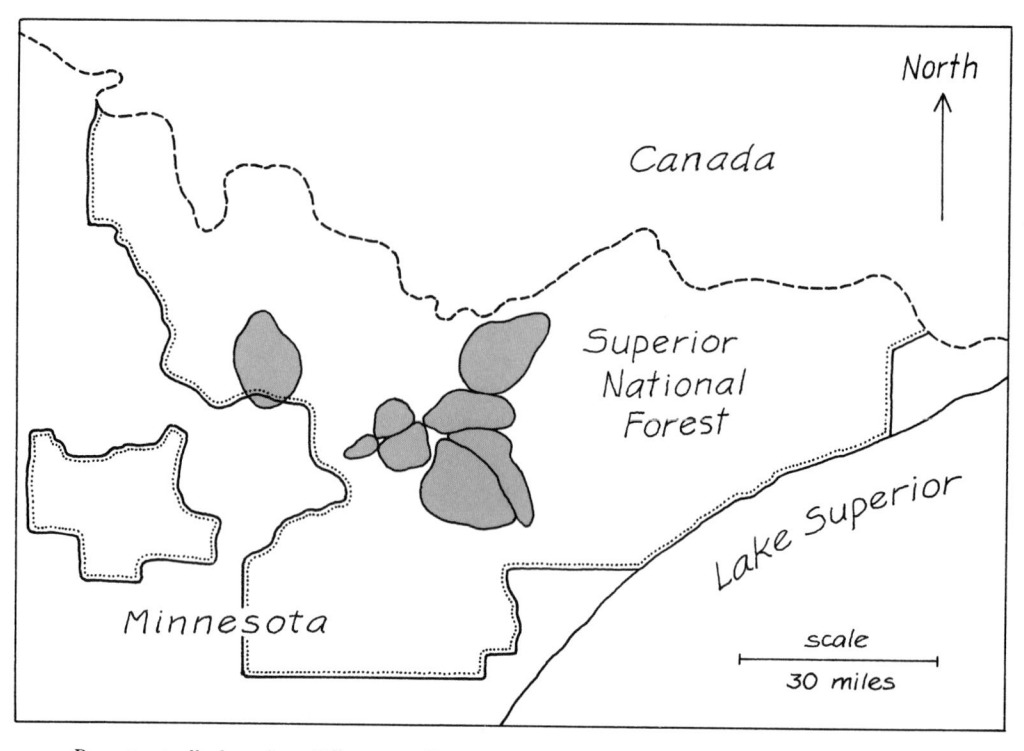

By repeatedly locating different radio-tagged wolves, Mech was able to mark the general territories (in gray) of eight wolf packs in part of the national forest.

can tell whether it is in its own territory. Each pack can quickly tell when it reaches the border of another pack's territory. And lone wolves can also tell whether they are in unoccupied territory, an occupied territory, or along the border between two packs."

These discoveries about the importance of scent marks led to further questions. If scent marks are territorial "advertisements," do lone wolves ever leave scent marks? If so, under what conditions? Dave Mech assigned another graduate student to investigate these questions. During two winters, Russel Rothman hiked on snowshoes along eighty miles of tracks left by lone wolves or by newly formed pairs of wolves. Since these were radio-tagged wolves, they could be located from an aircraft or a truck whenever conditions were good for Rothman to follow them and observe their scent-marking behavior.

He found that lone wolves pay close attention to the scent marks they find. They nuzzle or dig the snow in order to smell the odor, but they leave almost no scent marks themselves. They even seem to avoid leaving many scats along well-used wolf trails. This probably helps them avoid meeting a pack in its territory—a meeting that can be fatal for a lone wolf. One biologist actually saw a lone wolf find and sniff some scent marks of a pack. He said that the lone wolf "cowered and showed signs of anxiety."

By accident, another lone wolf came quite close to a sleeping pack. She stopped, lifted her head as though sniffing the air, then suddenly ran off. Apparently she had smelled fresh scent marks or the odor of the wolves themselves. The next day this radio-tagged wolf was found thirteen miles away. This story had a happy ending, though, as she found an unoccupied territory and a lone male wolf who became her mate.

Soon after two lone wolves form a pair they begin to leave many scent marks. In fact, both male and female mark the same places or objects with urine. This double mark is a signal that they are attempting to establish a territory. In well-established packs the alpha male and alpha female also leave double marks.

Russell Rothman and Dave Mech concluded that the presence or absence of a double mark might be important information for lone wolves entering a territory. In a small pack observed by Dave Mech, the alpha female was killed and there were no adult females to take her place. The alpha male continued to leave scent marks in the pack's territory but, of course, they were not the double marks of a mated pair.

"A female lone wolf eventually took the dead wolf's place," Mech reported. "She may have detected the absence of fresh double marks. From this she could determine that no other female was in the pack. Instead of fleeing from the vicinity of the pack, as a lone wolf usually would, this loner traveled parallel to the pack until she was eventually accepted as the alpha female."

Besides scent marks, wolves have another signaling system that helps them maintain their territories—howling. For centuries, people have wondered why wolves howl. It was once believed that they howled at

Wolves pay close attention to scent marks, which "advertise" pack territories and especially the borders of territories.

the moon. They don't. Adolph Murie and other observers learned that wolves may howl together when some pack members are leaving to hunt and howl again when the pack reunites. With Dave Mech's guidance, graduate student Fred Harrington tried to find out more about wolf howls.

Mech knew, from his experience and that of others, that humans can imitate wolf howls and induce wild wolves to reply. Mech himself and Canadian biologists have successfully led evening "howling" field trips for tourists, who are thrilled to hear a reply from a wild wolf. By combining human howls and radio tracking, Mech and Harrington were able to study wolf howling in a way that had not been possible before.

Using an antenna-equipped truck, they were able to locate specific packs and then approach within a mile or less. (Evidence shows that wolves can hear howling at a distance of more than five miles.) Thanks to radio tracking, the wolfmen already knew the packs well. Sometimes more than one pack member was radio-tagged. It was also possible for the wolfmen to use radio tracking to locate lone wolves or to approach wolves when they were known to be at or near a kill, to see how such wolves responded to howls.

Fred Harrington did most of the howling, and did it at night when he was certain that wolves were in hearing range. He howled in the same way and for the same number of minutes each time, then waited for a reply. If the wolves did not reply in a few minutes, he stopped howling to that pack for the night. Whether wolves did or did not reply, changes in radio signals revealed any wolf movements caused by the human howling.

After howling to seven different packs and to lone wolves almost 1,900 different times over a span of several months, Fred Harrington had some intriguing results. Wolves responded to his howls about 25 percent of the time, but lone wolves never replied, except when three of them were temporarily sharing a kill. When an individual wolf from a pack was alone, however, it sometimes howled back. Among the various packs, those with greater numbers and more adult members responded sooner than small packs with fewer adults.

In almost nine out of ten cases, when wolves did not respond to howling, they also moved *away* from the source of the howls. A pack did not usually move away, however, when it was at a kill or at a rendezvous site with pups. On a few occasions wolves from a pack came toward the human howler.

One night Fred Harrington and Dave Mech noticed that the signal of a radio-tagged wolf in a pack had become stronger and had changed direction. A few minutes later they heard two wolves moving within twenty-five feet of them in the forest. On three occasions when the identity of the approaching wolf was known (from its radio frequency), it was the alpha male of a pack.

From these results Harrington and Mech concluded that the wolves responded as though human howls came from strange wolves, not from fellow pack members. When a pack responded, it declared, "Here we are. This is our territory."

Understandably, not all wolves made this declaration. Lone wolves did not. Single wolves separated temporarily from their packs seldom

"This is our territory" is the message in a wolf pack's howls, which are most bold when the wolves are defending their pups or food.

advertised their position. Small packs were more cautious in howling than large packs, and these packs tended to draw back from the human howls they heard. The highest rate of response came from wolf packs that were at or near an animal they had killed or at a rendezvous site with pups. These are precious resources—hard-to-get food, or young that represent the pack's future. Wolves are most willing to defend, if necessary, their food and their pups.

Wolves usually try to avoid direct encounters with strange wolves. Scent marks help them to do this, and by howling, Harrington and Mech concluded, "Resident wolves advertise their position, allowing both resident and intruder to modify their movements to minimize the probability of accidentally meeting."

Under normal conditions, wolf messages of howls and scent marks work well, helping packs maintain their territories and avoid direct encounters with alien packs. But extraordinary conditions can change this, and Dave Mech's studies happened to coincide with a time of dramatic change in the environment of the wolves.

Deer are the main prey of wolves in Minnesota. Long before Dave Mech began radio-tracking wolves, deer numbers were declining in the Superior National Forest because of changes in vegetation. Aspen, an important deer food, was growing out of reach and also being replaced by balsam fir. Deer were not well nourished, and this reduced their reproduction.

The deer population was helped, however, by a series of mild winters. Then, from the winter of 1964–65 through the winter of 1971–72, seven of eight winters were severe. The winter of 1968–69 was the toughest on record, with extreme cold and extraordinary snowfall. The deer population was in big trouble. So, inevitably, was the wolf population.

Mild winters had helped the wolves maintain a fairly high population even though the deer had been gradually declining in most of the national forest. Conditions during the severe winter of 1968–69 made it easy for wolves to kill deer. They ate well, and breeding pairs produced litters of pups the following spring. The deer, on the other hand, reproduced poorly. Their numbers dropped sharply as the still-plentiful wolves continued to seek their main prey.

By the summer of 1972, deer were wiped out of a one thousand-square-mile area and were scarce in the surrounding region. Wolves sought other food. They killed many more beavers than usual. Some packs that formerly ignored moose began to hunt them. The wolves were under great stress and were desperate for food. They sought deer wherever they could find them, even if this meant trespassing into the territories of other packs.

As conflict between wolf packs increased, radio signals sometimes led Mech to wolves dead of starvation, or killed by other wolves in territorial fights.

A pair of wolves from the Harris Lake Pack left their territory, traveled sixteen miles through another territory and into a third territory. They killed a deer, ate it, and returned to their home range. Dave Mech watched from the air as another pack invaded a territory. The intruding wolves were excitedly on the trail of the resident wolves when a snowstorm and approaching darkness kept Mech from seeing whether there was a battle. The invading pack did, however, take over part of that territory for several weeks.

By 1972 the wolf population was dropping. Some young wolves starved to death. Analysis of blood samples from captured wolves showed that nearly all of them were malnourished. The lowest-ranking members of packs were in the poorest physical condition. Alpha wolves of packs continued to be the most healthy, but several of them were killed by other wolves in territorial fights.

It was a terrible time for deer, wolves, and, in some ways, for Dave Mech, who had a much-reduced wolf population to study. But he was grateful that he had begun his research when both deer and wolf numbers were fairly high and to have been able to witness and record the dramatic decline.

What would happen next? The answer to this question was of interest to scientists, to deer hunters, and to anyone curious about nature. Dave Mech hoped to answer it by continuing to observe the saga of the deer and the wolves.

8 Keeping Watch

Three deer walked into the clearing along a beaten path in the snow. They found hay and freshly cut aspen and began to feed. Then hidden rockets fired and projectiles carried a net over the deer, capturing them. Biologists came out of hiding, ready with radio collars for the deer. But why were wolfmen studying deer?

Dave Mech explained this step in his research: "As we answered more questions about the wolves, we realized that we didn't know enough about the deer on which they depended. We knew that the deer population had declined and not much more. So we began radio-tracking deer."

At first the deer were all captured in *yards*—areas where generation after generation of deer concentrate each winter. The four yards where deer were trapped were all found to be along the edges of wolf territories, but at first their location did not seem unusual.

One of the first discoveries by Mech and his assistants was that deer migrated long distances—as far as thirty-four miles—from their winter yards to their summer ranges. So the summer ranges of individual deer were scattered over a large area and were found in several wolf pack territories. Graduate student Reed Hoskinson prepared maps that showed the summer ranges of sixteen deer that he had radio-tracked. This led to an extraordinary finding.

"The greatest feeling of discovery I have had in twenty years of

To catch deer, biologists set off rockets (arrow points to one) that carry a strong net. Captured deer are then radio-tagged and released.

research," Mech wrote, "came in 1975 when I placed a graduate student's maps of individual deer ranges over my own plots of wolf pack territories: Almost all the deer studied lived along the very edges of wolf territories. I was elated at the surprising results. There was little chance that the findings were mere coincidence. . . . I suddenly saw the significance of the fact that the four yards where our deer had over-wintered all lay along wolf pack territory edges." He saw that "during the period of low deer density, most of the surviving deer inhabit wolf pack territory edges, both in summer and winter."

Further radio-tracking data from many deer confirmed this. But *why* do deer live along the borders of wolf territories? Is the food better there? Are deer able to sense where the edges of territories are and seek them out? Or do deer living along borders just survive better than those living in the centers of wolf territories?

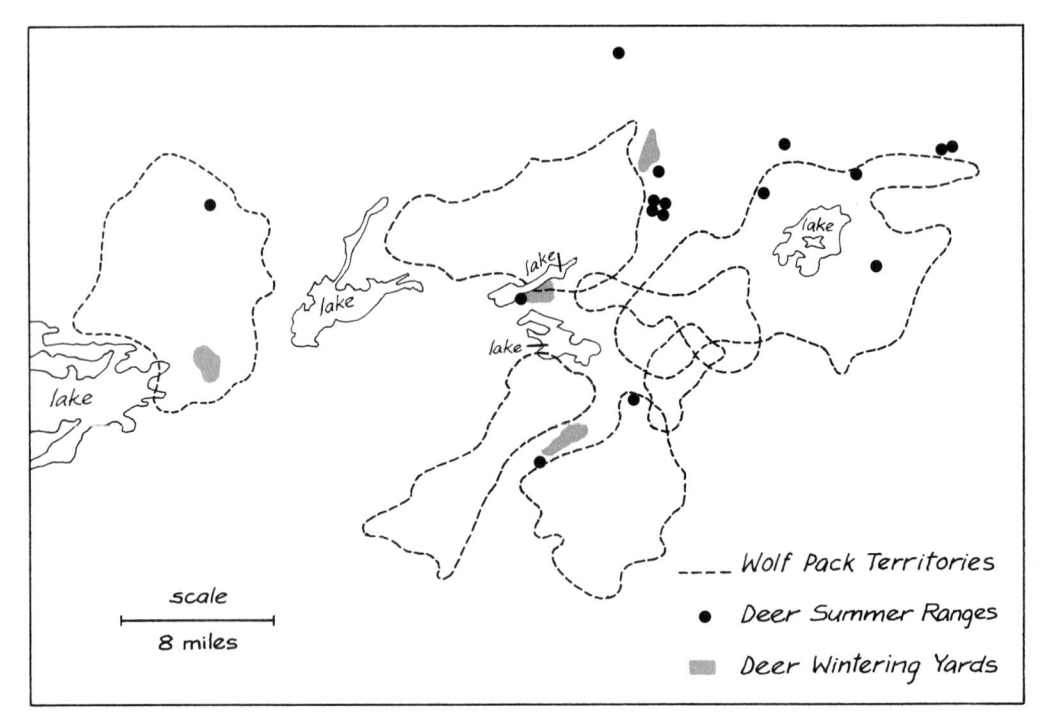

Putting maps of wolf pack and deer locations together, Mech found that deer seemed to survive best near the edge of pack territories or between territories.

The last possibility was most likely. From records of deer killed by wolves over the years, Mech could see that deer had lived throughout wolf territories before their population declined. As deer numbers dropped, wolves mostly killed deer near the centers of their territories. "In the Harris Lake Pack territory, for example," Mech reported, "only one of the twenty-seven kills I recorded for this pack during several winters was made in the territory edge."

Only when wolves became desperate for food did the Harris Lake Pack begin to kill deer along the edges of its territory. Other packs did, too. Even then, deer continued to survive and have long lives in these areas. The reason lies in the territorial life that is so basic to the survival of wolves.

Even under great stress, wolf packs tried to maintain their territories and to avoid direct conflict with other packs. The place of greatest danger of such conflict is along a territorial border. So wolves leave many scent marks there and do not use their territorial edges much. A buffer zone—one to two miles wide—exists between the territories of adjoining packs. This is wide enough to support numerous deer, summer or winter.

Dave Mech's studies of the locations of deer yards were unique because they were conducted in a region where wolves are still the major predators of deer. Other biologists had never considered wolves to be a factor in deer-yarding behavior because wolves no longer exist in most places where deer gather in yards, in northern states and in Canada. According to Dave Mech and another of his graduate students, Michael Nelson, wolves are one of the main reasons that deer gather in winter yards.

"By migrating to form a social group, deer are better able to escape from wolves. This sort of 'strength in numbers' behavior has been observed in many prey species—in schools of fish and in herds of antelope on the African plains, for example. It seems that deer can survive better as a group than they can alone, especially in winter, when they are most vulnerable. In places where there are no wolves today, deer continue to migrate to winter yards, still behaving in a way that once enabled deer populations to survive throughout their long, long relationship with wolves."

"I am fascinated," Mech added, "by the interactions between deer and wolves, by the ways in which the deer's life is geared to the wolf's, and vice versa. We've only begun to understand this."

About 1974 the deer population of the Superior National Forest stopped its decline and remained stable at a low level. The deer living in territory buffer zones were a reservoir from which deer might eventually repopulate the entire region. Dave Mech kept a close watch on the deer population in order to be able to record the comeback if and when it happened.

The numbers of wolves also declined to a low level. There were more trespassing incidents and battles in which wolves died. One pack broke up when its alpha female starved to death. All wolves were underweight. Few pups were born, and many of them died during their first winter. Still, it seemed that the wolves had partly adjusted to the low deer population and would not dwindle much further.

"If the deer population starts to rise," Dave Mech said, "we will be watching the wolf population to see when it begins to respond. We think there will be a time lag and that the deer will be able to build for several years before we see a response in the wolf population."

Since 1977, Mech and other scientists have kept a captive wolf colony near St. Paul. Remembering his experience with Lightning, he insisted that the wolves be given numbers, not names, so that students, staff members, and he would not forget that the wolves were research animals, not pets. The wolves are well cared for. Keeping them is the only way to get some basic information about wolf reproduction and about the normal levels of hormones, nutrients, and other substances found in wolf blood. Once the normal levels of such substances are known, the levels measured in blood samples taken from wild wolves will have more meaning.

Dave Mech continued to write about his findings in science journals. He was concerned, however, about the possible effects of one report. In 1977, he coauthored a report called *The Role of the Wolf in a Deer Decline in the Superior National Forest,* knowing that the information in it could be used—or misused—against wolves. Some deer hunters and other people have long believed that wolves are always on the verge of killing off all deer. On the basis of the report, wolf haters could say, "We told you so." It could also serve to justify their calls for the extermination or control of wolves.

Nevertheless, Mech had the report published. He said, "I am basically a researcher, and I feel I have to reveal everything I learn. It was a story that had to be told because it was another piece in the puzzle of wolf ecology.

"In general, predators don't have harmful effects on prey popula-

Captive wolves are temporarily knocked out so that blood and urine samples and other information about their health can be obtained for later study.

tions. It makes sense: The survival of predators depends on the survival of their prey. But most studies have been done when the prey were fairly abundant. Such prey populations can recover from a temporary decline caused by bad weather or some other harmful factor in their environment.

"The circumstances I found were quite different—a deer population already in decline because of dwindling food, a string of hard winters, and a high predator population. This unusual *combination* of factors caused the deer population to crash. And wolves definitely contributed to the crash.

"This story needed to be told, simply because it is a different story, a special case, and the truth. And revealing the truth is part of my job as a scientist."

Dave Mech's commitment to finding and telling the truth about wolves has caused some people to call him prowolf and others to call him antiwolf. It has also added to his credibility with both sides.

Wolves still hold many secrets for Dave Mech. He wants to know more about how packs form and what happens to individuals in them. Why do some pack members leave while others stay? What happens to the wolves that leave? Many more years of radio tracking may help answer these questions.

Continuation of this research will also reveal more about wolf territories and population changes, because Mech's study is unique in the world. Most wolf research projects (and those of many other wild species) have only enough funds to last a few years. The Isle Royale project has continued more than twenty years, but conclusions from it are influenced and somewhat limited by its special island circumstances. Mech's investigations cover a much larger area and many more wolves.

Even though Mech's research is comparatively well funded, his staff is small. There aren't enough openings for the college graduates who would like to study wolves. One young wildlife biologist worked as an unpaid volunteer for a year, supporting himself by tending bar at night. Some former graduate students managed to find projects related to their experience in Minnesota—Fred Harrington is studying captive wolves in Canada, and Roger Peters is studying coyotes in Colorado. Overall, there aren't many opportunities in the world to study wolves, and Dave Mech feels privileged to be a wolfman.

Considering that he began like Adolph Murie, one man alone in the wilderness, picking up wolf scats, he has come a long way. His expertise about wolves and radio tracking has taken him as a consultant to Africa, India, Italy, Spain, and the Soviet Union. He is the author or coauthor of scores of scientific reports. Yet he doesn't flaunt his authority or his accomplishments.

Wolf and wolfman—the alpha male of a captive wolf pack nuzzles the hand of Dave Mech.

At project headquarters in the north country, he is not "Dr. Mech" but simply "Dave." The mood in the building is informal. One person makes a sandwich, while in a nearby room another dissects a dead wolf. In the refrigerator, containers of blood samples stand beside beer bottles. Staff and students come and go, work on radio receivers and other equipment, discuss the day's events and the next day's plans.

Whether they talk about wolves, ravens, or snowshoe hares, there is a common attitude, a tone set by Dave Mech. There is excitement about knowledge and a dedication to seeking it. And it seems like a good and honorable thing, to ask questions and to pursue your curiosity about life, about nature, and especially about wolves.

Further Reading

Allen, Durward L. *Wolves of Minong: Their Vital Role in a Wild Community.* Boston: Houghton Mifflin Company, 1979. A detailed account of eighteen years of research on the wolves, moose, beavers, foxes, and other wildlife of Isle Royale, well illustrated and enriched with many personal anecdotes.

Allen, Durward, and Mech, L. David. "Wolves versus Moose on Isle Royale." *National Geographic,* February 1963, pp. 200–19. A heavily illustrated account of Dave Mech's research on Isle Royale.

Barry, Scott. *The Kingdom of Wolves.* New York: G. P. Putnam's Sons, 1979. An introduction to wolf biology and behavior, illustrated with many black-and-white photos.

Harrington, Fred H., and Mech, L. David. "Wolf Howling and Its Role in Territory Maintenance." *Behaviour,* volume 68, number 3, pp. 207–49. Describes the responses of wolves to about 1,900 tests using human howls, and draws conclusions about how howling helps wolves advertise and maintain their territories.

Lopez, Barry H. *Of Wolves and Men.* New York: Charles Scribner's Sons, 1978. This well written book dwells for a time on present knowledge of wolves but probes deeply into Native American attitudes toward wolves and the origins and effects of centuries of wolf hatred.

McNamee, Thomas. "Trouble in Wolf Heaven." *Audubon,* January 1982, pp. 84–95. A recent account of wolf and moose population dynamics on Isle Royale.

Mech, L. David. "Where Can the Wolf Survive?" *National Geographic,* October 1977, pp. 518–37. A brief summary of facts known about wolves, including their range and behavior, and attitudes about them. Illustrated with extraordinary color photographs.

Mech, L. David. "Why Some Deer Are Safe from Wolves." *Natural History,* January 1979, pp. 71–77. How and why buffer zones between wolf territories are relatively safe places for deer.

Mech, L. David. *The Wolf: The Ecology and Behavior of an Endangered Species.* New York: Natural History Press, 1970 (also available in a paperback edition, published by the University of Minnesota Press). Dedicated to Adolph Murie, this book is the first attempt at a complete account of the biology and behavior of the wolf. Although Mech and other wolfmen have learned more about the wolf since this book was written, it is still the most definitive and authoritative book on the subject.

Mech, L. David. *The Wolves of Isle Royale.* Fauna of the National Parks, Fauna Series 7. Washington, D.C.: U.S. Government Printing Office, 1966. Mech's report on his Isle Royale studies includes details of many wolf-moose encounters and is illustrated with more than one hundred black-and-white photos.

Mech, L. David, and Karns, Patrick D. *The Role of the Wolf in a Deer Decline in the Superior National Forest.* USDA Forest Service Research Paper NC-148. St. Paul, Minnesota: North Central Experiment Station, 1977. A twenty-four-page report on the drop in deer numbers brought about by a combination of bad weather, a worsening food situation, and wolf predation.

Mowat, Farley. *Never Cry Wolf.* Boston: Little, Brown, 1963 (also available in paperback editions, published by Dell and Bantam). Although published as nonfiction, Mowat's book seems to be fiction based mostly on the experiences of Adolph Murie and other biologists. Nevertheless, this tale of one man's adventures with Arctic wolves conveys a strong appreciation of wolves and their role in nature.

Murie, Adolph. *The Wolves of Mount McKinley.* Fauna of the National Parks, Fauna Series 5. Washington, D.C.: U.S. Government Printing Office, 1944. Murie's detailed account of his pioneer study of wolves in Alaska.

Peters, Roger R., and Mech, L. David. "Scent Marking in Wolves." *American Scientist,* November–December 1975, pp. 628–37. Details of the scent-marking studies of Peters and Mech, and their conclusions about the function of scent marking in wolf territorial behavior.

Rothman, Russell J., and Mech, L. David. "Scent Marking in Lone Wolves and Newly Formed Pairs." *Animal Behavior,* volume 27, number 3, 1979, pp. 750–60. This journal article describes how scent-marking behavior of lone wolves changes when they form pairs.

Rutter, Russell J., and Pimlott, Douglas H. *The World of the Wolf.* Philadelphia: Lippincott, 1968. Written by Canadian biologists, this fine introduction to the wolf's life is illustrated with many black-and-white photos. It also tells of a family's funny and tragic experiences with tame wolves.

Zimen, Erik. *The Wolf: A Species in Danger.* New York: Delacorte Press, 1980. A German scientist describes his observations of the behavior of captive wolves and studies of wild wolves in Italy.

Index

Asterisk (*) indicates illustration

A
Adirondack State Park, 8–9
Africa, 19–20, 61, 64
Alaska, 2–4, 5, 29, 36, 37
Allen, Dr. Durward, 9, 14
American Wildlife, 5
Arctic, 6, 19
Arctic Wild, 36
aspen, 12, 55, 58

B
bears, 2, 8*, 9, 39
beavers, 10, 56
Birch Lake Pack, 49
Boundary Waters Canoe Area, 37
Boy Scouts, 6

C
Canada, 4, 9, 25, 43, 52, 61, 64
caribou, 2, 3*
Catskill Mountains, 6
Cole, James, 9
Como Zoo, 30, 36

Cornell University, 6, 7–9, 14
coyotes, 9, 64
Crisler, Lois, 36

D
deer, *see* wolf relationships with deer
deer hunters, 57, 62
deer yards, 58, 59, 60*, 61
Denali Park and Preserve, 2
Douglas, William O., 36

E
Eskimos, 1–2
European settlers, 1–2

F
Federal Endangered Species Act, 44
foxes, 6, 7

H
Harrington, Fred, 52–55, 64
Harris Lake Pack, 45, 46, 49, 57, 60

69

Index

Hoskinson, Reed, 58
Hunt's Hill, 6

I
Indians, 1–2
Isle Royale National Park, 4, 5, 9, 10–11*, 12–13*, 14–19, 21–28, 29, 37, 42, 64
Italy, 4, 64

J
Jeff White: Young Woodsman, 5–6

L
Lake Superior, 5, 11*
Lightning, 31–32, 33*, 34–35*, 36, 62; *see also* wolf pups

M
Macalester College, 29
Mech, Betty Ann, 13–14, 19, 21, 29, 35*
Mech, David:
  aerial observations of, 14–18, 21–22, 23*, 24, 25*, 26, 27*, 28, 38*, 41, 42, 45, 47, 57
  and airsickness, 14–15
  and back injury, 21
  and pet wolves, 30*, 31–32, 34–36, 47
  as wolfman, 4, 43, 64–65*
  at Cornell University, 7, 8*, 9
  childhood of, 5–7*
  children of, 29
  Isle Royale studies of, 10–11*, 12–17*, 18–19, 21–28

radio-tracking studies of, 29, 37, 39, 40*, 41–44*, 45–46, 50, 53, 56*, 64
Michigan, 4, 21
Minnesota, 4, 11*, 29, 30, 37, 39*, 41, 55, 64
moose, 9, 10, 12–13, 15, 16, 17*, 18, 19, 21–22, 23, 24, 25*, 26, 27*, 28, 32, 37, 56; *see also* wolf relationships with moose
Mount McKinley National Park, 2
mountain sheep, 2, 13
Murie, Adolph, 2–4, 5, 13, 52, 64
Murray, Don, 14, 15, 21, 22, 23, 24, 26

N
National Park Service, 9, 10, 12
National Science Foundation, 9
Nelson, Michael, 61
New York Zoological Society, 43

P
Peters, Roger, 49, 64
Purdue University, 9, 14, 18

R
radio tracking, *see* Mech, David, radio-tracking studies
ravens, 47, 65
Role of the Wolf in a Deer Decline in the Superior National Forest, The, 62
Rothman, Russell, 50–51

S
Shelton, Phillip, 28
snowshoeing, 8, 15, 17, 21, 22, 37, 50

Superior National Forest, 11*, 37, 38*, 45, 46, 50*, 55, 61
Syracuse, New York, 5-6

T

Thunder, 31-32, 33*, 36; see also Mech, David, and pet wolves
trapping, 6-7, 39; see also wolf trapping

U

United States Fish and Wildlife Service, 43
United States Forest Service, 46
University of Minnesota, 29

W

We Took to the Woods, 5
wolf:
  adult behavior, 4, 14, 15, 16*, 19, 20*, 21-23*, 24-25*, 26, 27*, 32, 33, 36, 39, 40, 41-42*, 43, 45-46, 47, 48*, 49, 51, 52*, 53, 54*, 55-57, 60-61, 62, 64
  alpha, 32, 45, 49, 51, 54, 57, 62, 65*
  attitudes toward, 1-2, 12, 22, 24, 26, 34, 62
  captive colony, 62, 63*
  dens, 3-4, 43, 47
  howling, 23, 29, 51-54*, 55
  lone, 41, 50-51, 53
  number 1051, 42
  number 2407, 45-46, 47
  populations, 15, 28, 37, 47, 55-57, 61-62, 64
  pups, 3-4, 28, 30*-32, 33*, 34-36, 43, 47, 53, 55, 56, 62
  ranges, 2, 41
  relationships with deer, 37, 41-42, 47, 49, 55-60*, 61-63
  relationships with moose, 9, 12, 13, 15, 16-18, 21-22, 25*, 26-28, 56
  scats, 2, 5, 10, 13, 14, 19, 51, 64
  scent marks, 49-51, 52*, 55, 61
  territories, 41, 43, 46, 47, 49-50*, 51, 54-55, 56-57, 58-60*, 61, 64
  tracks, 3, 9, 10, 12, 14, 19, 49, 50
  trapping, 39, 44, 45, 46
  travels, 15, 24, 25-26, 42, 43, 51
Wolf, The: The Ecology and Behavior of an Endangered Species, 36
Wolves of Isle Royale, The, 29
Wolves of Mount McKinley, The, 4